DISCOVER DOGS WITH THE AMERICAN CANINE ASSOCIATION

I LIKE

AIREDALE TERRIERS!

Linda Bozzo

Published in 2018 by Enslow Publishing, LLC.
101 W. 23rd Street, Suite 240, New York, NY 10011

Library of Congress Cataloging-in-Publication Data

Names: Bozzo, Linda, author.
Title: I like Airedale terriers! / Linda Bozzo.
Description: New York, NY : Enslow Publishing, 2018. | Series: Discover dogs with the American Canine Association | Includes bibliographical references and index. | Audience: Grades K to 3.
Identifiers: LCCN 2017006753| ISBN 9780766091214 (library bound) | ISBN 9780766091191 (pbk.) | ISBN 9780766091207 (6 pack)
Subjects: LCSH: Airedale terrier—Juvenile literature.
Classification: LCC SF429.A6 B69 2017 | DDC 636.755—dc23
LC record available at https://lccn.loc.gov/2017006753

Printed in China

To Our Readers: We have done our best to make sure all websites in this book were active and appropriate when we went to press. However, the author and the publisher have no control over and assume no liability for the material available on those websites or on any websites they may link to. Any comments or suggestions can be sent by email to customerservice@enslow.com.

Photo Credits: Cover, p. 1 Dmitry Kalinovsky/Shutterstock.com; pp. 3 (left), 21 Anneka/Shutterstock.com; p. 3 (right) David Havel/Shutterstock.com; p. 5 Gina Callaway/Shutterstock.com; p. 6 NEstudio/Shutterstock.com; p. 9 Hero Images/Getty Images; p. 10 Lenkadan/Shutterstock.com; p. 13 (puppy) Samoilova Helen/Shutterstock.com; p. 13 (collar) graphicphoto/iStock/Thinkstock, (bed) Luisa Leal Photography/Shutterstock.com, (brush) In-Finity/Shutterstock.com, (food and water bowls) exopixel/Shutterstock.com, (leash, toys) © iStockphoto.com/Liliboas; p. 14 Tierfotoagentur/Alamy Stock Photo; p. 17 Krakozawr/E+/Getty Images; p. 18 FatCamera/E+/Getty Images; p. 19 altrendo images/Juice Images/Getty Images.

Enslow Publishing
101 W. 23rd Street
Suite 240
New York, NY 10011
USA
enslow.com

CONTENTS

IS AN AIREDALE TERRIER RIGHT FOR YOU?

Airedale terriers can make great family pets. This breed is not best for apartment living. If you have a large fenced yard, an Airedale may be right for you.

As the largest of all the terriers, the Airedale terrier is known as the "King of Terriers."

A DOG OR A PUPPY?

Airedale puppies do well with most training. But training any puppy takes time. If you do not have time to train a puppy, you may want an older Airedale instead.

Airedale terriers can act like puppies well into their adult lives.

LOVING YOUR AIREDALE TERRIER

Loving your Airedale will keep her happy. Cuddle her. Play with her. Give her treats. Airedales enjoy life most when they are by your side.

EXERCISE

Airedales enjoy long walks or jogging with you on a **leash**. They like to do tricks and play games like **fetch**.

Airedales have been known to tire out their owners!

FEEDING YOUR AIREDALE TERRIER

Airedales can be fed wet or dry dog food. Ask a **veterinarian (vet)**, a doctor for animals, which food is best for your dog and how much to feed her.

Give your Airedale fresh, clean water every day. Remember to keep your dog's food and water dishes clean. Dirty dishes can make a dog sick.

Do not feed your dog people food. It can make her sick.

Your new dog will need:

a collar with a tag

a bed

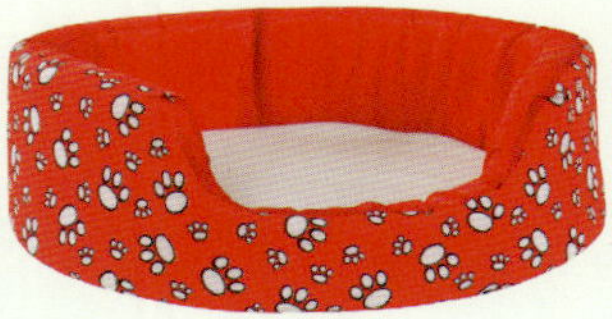

a brush

food and water dishes

a leash

toys

The Airedale terrier's coat has two layers: a topcoat, which is dense and wiry, and an undercoat, which is short and soft.

GROOMING

These medium-sized dogs don't **shed** often. This means their hair doesn't fall out as much as other breeds. Brushing your Airedale will help keep him clean and looking his best. Some pet owners like to get their Airedales' coats trimmed by a **groomer**.

Your dog will need a bath every so often. Use a gentle soap made just for dogs. An Airedale's nails will need to be clipped. A vet or groomer can show you how. Your dog's ears should be cleaned, and his teeth should be brushed by an adult.

WHAT YOU SHOULD KNOW

If bored, Airedales can get into trouble.

They are not good in a house with small pets.

This breed likes to dig, chase, and bark.

Airedales make good watch dogs.

You will need to take your new dog to the vet for a checkup. He will need shots, called **vaccinations**, and yearly checkups to keep him healthy. If you think your dog may be sick or hurt, call your vet.

A GOOD FRIEND

This silly dog will be a fun-loving friend for many years. Airedales can live as long as 10 to 14 years.

NOTE TO PARENTS

It is important to consider having your dog spayed or neutered when the dog is young. Spaying and neutering are operations that prevent unwanted puppies and can help improve the overall health of your dog.

It is also a good idea to microchip your dog, in case he or she gets lost. A vet will implant a microchip under the skin containing an identification number that can be scanned at a vet's office or animal shelter. The microchip registry is contacted, and the company uses the ID number to look up your information from a database.

Some towns require licenses for dogs, so be sure to check with your town clerk.

For more information, speak with a vet.

There are many dogs, young and old, waiting to be adopted from animal shelters and rescue groups.

Words to Know

fetch To go after a toy and bring it back.

groomer A person who bathes and brushes dogs.

leash A chain or strap that attaches to the dog's collar.

shed When dog hair falls out so new hair can grow.

vaccinations Shots that dogs need to stay healthy.

veterinarian (vet) A doctor for animals.

Read About Dogs

Books

Carney, Elizabeth. *Woof! 100 Fun Facts About Dogs.* Washington, DC: National Geographic Children's Books, 2017.

Gagne, Tammy. *West Highlands, Scotties, and Other Terriers.* North Mankato, MN: Capstone Press, 2016.

Murray, Julie. *Dogs.* Minneapolis, MN: Abdo Kids, 2015.

Websites

American Canine Association Inc., Kids Corner
www.acakids.com

Visit the official website of the American Canine Association.

National Geographic for Kids, Pet Central
kids.nationalgeographic.com/explore/pet-central/

Learn more about dogs and other pets at the official site of the National Geographic Society for Kids.

INDEX